I used a Flat Sable brush # 14, Round Bristle brushes # 1 and 2. Center of roses: Alizarin and Red. Deep red roses: Alizarin and Red. Darkest part under roses: Alizarin, Cobalt Blue, and Cadmium Red. Pink rose: Red and Yellow with much more White added, some Green to dull. Leaves: Cadmium Red, Cobalt Blue, Cadmium Yellow, and some Viridian. Background: Ochre, Cobalt Blue, Cad. Yellow Medium, and Cad. Red. Background is cool on one side and warm on the other with a light center. Try to keep cool colors next to warm colors and weak colors next to strong colors. Work from dark to light.

For Pink-Orange petals use Cad. Red Light and Cad. Yel. Medium, shaded with Aliz. Crimson and Ultra. Blue. Roses: Cad. Yel. Medium and Raw Sienna. Pink centers: Cad. Red Light shading to Cad. Yel. Medium and Raw Sienna. Background: Ultra. Blue, Cad. Yel. Medium, and Burnt Sienna. Leaves: Ultra. Blue and Cad. Yel. Medium, adding Aliz. Crimson or Cad. Red Light for the edges. Suggest the centers with little dots of Burnt Sienna. Use a tiny small Sable brush for this. Try different mixtures until you can match the shades of the roses.

FLUORESCENT ROSES. The colors in these roses seemed to change with different positions. One has a pink center—the other a pale Yellow. Always vary the sizes and shapes of roses in a painting, it is more interesting. Study rose leaves; learn to draw them in all positions, put flat-toned ones in the background. Vary their size and their colors, notice the effect of light and shade on them. Look for very subtle colors then mix color to match as closely as you can. Observe the tender little leaves just budding out, a little spray of them adds variety to the painting.

Colors used are Ultramarine Blue, Alizarin Crimson, Cadmium Lemon, and Raw Sienna. Mix Alizarin Crimson and Ultra. Blue with a tiny bit of Lemon for the Black teapot and paint it first. Use Raw Sienna and Lemon Yellow with a tiny bit of Blue for roses, their centers are mainly Raw Sienna. Leaf colors are Yellow and Blue mixed, this makes a pretty Green. Alizarin Crimson and Lemon Yellow are mixed for the very centers. When you are completely through with the painting, put one little brush stroke of Orange behind the stems. Always add White to make the right values.

YELLOW ROSES IN BLACK TEAPOT. These colors are good if you are a beginner because you can learn to mix the primary colors, Red, Blue, and Yellow. If you are buying paints for the first time this painting will save you money. Background: Red, Blue, and Yellow mixed, with White added. Lightest parts of roses are mostly White with a little Yellow added. The little teapot is a family heirloom, I remember my mother using it when I was a child on a Kansas farm. You probably have a nice antique pitcher, pot, vase, an old sugar bowl, etc., that would look good with roses in it.

Colors are Perm. Grn. Light, Cad. Yel. Medium, Cad. Yel. Light, Orange, Burnt Sienna, Raw Sienna, Aliz. Crimson, and Ultra. Blue. After you sketch in your painting put in dark leaves as indicated, using Perm. Grn. Light and Burnt Sienna mixed in a dark value. You can go over darks later with lighter colors easier than going over lights with darks. Dark rose: Yellow, Raw Sienna, Burnt Sienna, and a little Orange. Yellow rose: Raw Sienna, Yel. Medium, and White. Rose hips: Burnt Sienna, and Orange; stems: Burnt Sienna. Background: Green, Aliz. Crimson, Burnt Sienna, and White.

YELLOW GOLD ROSES. This would make a very pretty painting to hang in a room with yellow or gold accents. It is also a good seller. People can't seem to resist yellow roses, they are so cheerful. I made these up in my mind and arranged them in a decorative style. Remember, on these roses to keep the centers dark. As you learn to paint roses from this book think of some other arrangements and add other colors if you wish. If you find it too difficult to mix colors, use the ones already prepared in tubes. You might find it easier. I do both.

I used a small round brush to sketch the entire picture. If you wish use a wash on your canvas first, I often do, this helps tone down a too-white canvas. Charcoal or pencil may be used to block in but be sure to use a fixative afterwards or the black will bleed into your colors. If you like to paint tiny miniatures a pencil is best to sketch with. At times I use Bristle brushes—sometimes Sable. Some are flat and wide, others are small and round. I use the brush most suitable for the size stroke needed. I seldom use Black but mix my own if I do.

HELEN'S ROSE IN A BLUE VASE. A friend of mine who grows different kinds of beautiful roses invited me to choose any I needed for this book. I thought this one was very beautiful. If you are unable to finish your painting in one day, put the roses in water in the refrigerator over night. They will stay fresh this way for several days. I put a light over these to see the shadows and highlights. Look carefully at the colors of roses for they are very subtle. Once you have painted a pretty rose, it won't wither as would a garden one and you will have it to look at for many years.

Colors used are Cadmium Red Deep, Perm. Green Light, Alizarin, Cerulean Blue, Raw Sienna, and Cad. Yellow Medium. Leaves are Perm. Green Light, Cad. Red Deep, and Cad. Yellow Medium. Roses are Cad. Red Deep and White with some Cad. Red Light in the center of the roses. Add a tiny bit of Yellow to White for the lightest part of the cup of the rose. Keep leaves dull Gray-Green. Background—Red-Green and Cerulean Blue and White. By keeping all colors light and about the same value results in a very delicate painting. This is an easy composition to start on.

DELICATE ROSES. Follow the step drawings on opposite page. Block in your composition carefully and study it for balance. This is a very important part of any painting; your colors and tonal values may be perfect but if your composition is unbalanced it will ruin the entire painting. I put a lot of effort into moving the flowers into different positions until I am satisfied with them. Always feel free to change any of these paintings to suit your purpose. This would be very nice in Golds and Yellows, also. There are many colors of roses from deepest Reds to palest pastels.

After sketching in your composition lay in your background with Ultramarine Blue, Cadmium Red Light, Cadmium Yellow Medium, Cadmium Lemon, Alizarin Crimson, and Yellow Ochre. Add Raw Sienna and White for the lights. Roses are Yellow Ochre, Alizarin Crimson, and Ultra. Blue. Highlights are Cadmium Lemon and White. When painting glass, use very light crisp strokes for the highlights, putting them on last. Use a tiny round brush. This was a very beautiful rose and I painted the colors as closely as possible.

STILL LIFE IN GLASS VASE. As background I used a dark cloth drape. With a spotlight on the roses, they stood out nicely, being light in color. Here are three stages of bloom—a bud, a half-opened rose, and one in full bloom. The colors are very delicate, and the leaves are copied true to color. I borrowed the vase from my friend Sally, it was just what I needed. I like to paint glass and really enjoyed this one. Learn to copy first, then later you can vary your paintings. This is a good lesson in light and dark contrasts.

Sketch in your composition with a round Bristle brush. The canvas is 16x20. You may use a Flat Sable or Flat Bristle # 12 or larger to fill in the color if desired. Center of red rose: Cad. Red Deep and Ultra. Blue. Cad. Red Light and Ultra. Blue for center of the pink roses. For the lighter shades, use Red and Ultra. Blue and more White, or Red and Green and White. Background is Ultra. Blue, Raw Sienna, Cadmium Red Lt., Viridian, and Yellow Ochre. Add Cad. Yellow and White for lighter shades of Pink, Red, and Green.

WALL CORSAGE. I attended an art demonstration once and the artist said, "The first thing we need when we start to paint is enthusiasm." I would like to go even a step farther and say, "If we lack enthusiasm and become discouraged, go ahead and try anyway, and as you paint you will enjoy it and forget your troubles. Perhaps you will end up being enthusiastic in spite of yourself. You don't have to be a good artist to have fun painting." I know this works for I have tried it. We all tend to procrastinate—it is very easy to do.

FRONT AND CENTER ROSES. Finish sketch-lay in darks. This is a warm painting, so cool color in white rose and vase stand out. Gold handles on vase: Cad. Yel. Medium and Raw Sienna. Real leaves were green but I changed them to Brown. It's fun doing things you feel like doing. I paint by feeling and keep trying until I am satisfied. Keep dull colors in background; bright ones will then stand out. I had admired this antique vase so many times that my friend Blanche gave it to me to keep, so I was very happy and inspired when I painted this and will enjoy it many times with different floral arrangements.

LOLA ADES
'70

First sketch flowers, leaves, and vase. The color of the daisies is White with Blue added. The centers are Burnt Sienna. The vase is Yellow Ochre and Blue. Add dark leaves—colors are Blue, Yellow, and Burnt Sienna. Save the detail until last and finish with dark accents and highlights. Add a touch of Orange in the vase for reflections of background; also reflections of Yellow as the vase has a shiny finish and has many reflections. Blue is Cobalt Blue. Mix Blue and Yellow for Green. Don't forget to add buds for variety.

BLUE DAISIES. Almost anyone would like a daisy painting as a gift. They are the next most popular seller after roses, you will probably find them easier to paint, too. Daisies make wonderful miniature paintings, they can be painted in almost any color and blend in well with other flowers. Roses and daisies are very pretty together; use them in backgrounds for other flowers, just **suggest** them, don't try to paint every petal or they will look as though you pasted them on. Subtly blend or "feather" the outer petals into your background color.

Deep red ranunculas: Red and Ultra. Blue. Rose Red for pink one with a little Orange to warm it in spots. Orange ones are Cadmium Yellow Medium, Orange, and Cadmium Red in different mixtures. Pitcher is mostly Blue and White with Cadmium Yellow to warm it. For background use Cadmium Yellow, Red, and Cobalt Blue with White. Mix Yellow and Blue for Green colors. I added small flowers for softening effect. Burnt Umber and Cobalt Blue for center of flowers. Note shadows and highlights in the flowers.

RANUNCULAS. Ranunculas are one of my favorite flowers. I especially like the Black centers in contrast to the vivid colors of the flowers. I arranged them in the vase until I had a pleasing composition. They give the impression of being very fragile and might wilt very quickly, however, they are quite sturdy and will hold up remarkably well for a still life. You can add sprigs of tiny flowers to balance and enhance the bouquet. Follow the step drawings and colors and the result will be beautiful.

My palette is Cadmium Red, Cadmium Yellow Medium, Cadmium Lemon, Alizarin Crimson, Orange, Rose Red, Ultra. Blue, and Cobalt Blue. White flowers have Rose Red around edges and have so many other subtle, muted colors that there is no pure White in them; they just **appear** White. Use a little Blue in shadows and Yellow in highlights. The red ones are Cadmium Red and Alizarin Crimson. Add Yellow in warm spots. Blur the edges with your finger or a spot brush. This still life consists of just the flowers without vase, pitcher, or bowl.

MRS. B'S RANUNCULAS. The lady that gave me these lived in another town. I had never met her but was told she had all kinds of flowers and would be glad to give me some. It was true, her home was surrounded with all kinds of flowers. I couldn't resist this bunch of beauties and hurried right home and went to work. I tried to paint them as they appeared in the garden sunlight. These colors were as close as possible to the actual colors of the flowers. I chose the largest and prettiest two for the center of interest.

FIRST PRIZE ROSES. I had no live roses to study when I painted these; they are imaginary. If you have none, and cannot get any, this shows what you can achieve merely by remembering the structure and colors of a rose. The contrasts are strong in this painting. **Think** how the buds look, also, don't forget to add some thorns. Colors of roses: Vermilion and White, a little Yellow and Viridian, and Burnt Sienna. Leaves are Viridian, Burnt Sienna, Cad. Yel. Medium, and Cad. Lemon. Background: Burnt Umber, Burnt Sienna, Viridian, and Alizarin. Again I used no container or vase.

MEMORY LANE ROSES. Notice a rose has a cup in the center. The leaves or petals around it open gradually and fall backwards on the outside. These remind me of long ago, sort of an old-fashioned bouquet. Background: Cobalt Blue, Raw Sienna, Burnt Sienna, Cad. Yellow, and Alizarin Crimson. Pink rose: Cad. Red Deep, Alizarin, Cobalt Blue. Yellow rose: Orange, Raw Sienna, Burnt Sienna, Cobalt Blue, and Cad. Yel. Deep. White rose: Burnt Sienna, Cad. Yellow, and Cobalt Blue. Leaves: Burnt Sienna, Aliz. Crimson, Cobalt Blue, Orange, and Viridian.

GARDEN BOUQUET. Be sure to mold the shape of the flower. Roses are a "layered" flower, the petals lie, one upon another, in a wonderful, symmetrical, and unbelievable product of Mother Nature. They unfold from tightly closed buds to a fragrant and dazzling brilliance of no other flower. If you have grown roses, remember the beauty and perfection of an opening bud with drops of morning dew clinging to it's petals. In painting, keep in mind the source of light—dark on one side, coming to light on the other. Tonal values are very important so study them carefully.

ONE DOZEN ROSES. I was thinking of an old song when I arranged this one. So I'm sending you "One dozen roses" to paint. Put your heart into it and give it to someone you love, they will love you for it. The two white roses are the **Center of Interest.** The background is Cad. Yel. Medium, Yel. Ochre, Cad. Red Medium, Alizarin, and Cobalt Blue. Dark brown leaves are Alizarin, Cad. Lemon, Raw Sienna, and Cobalt Blue. Pink roses: Vermilion and White, Cobalt, Yel. Ochre, Cad. Lemon Yellow. Red roses: Cad. Red Medium, Alizarin, and Vermilion. Yellow roses: Yellow and Raw Sienna.

FADED ROSES. I call these roses **Faded** for they were painted mainly with earth colors, with exceptions of Blue, Orange, and Lem. Yellow. I had never seen roses like these; the petals were pointed and rolled back like scrolls and were a soft Brownish-Yellow. They took much study and careful observation and are for a more advanced student. Colors used with White: Naples Yellow, Indian Red, Gr. Earth, Yel. Ochre, Payne's Grey, Orange, Burnt Sienna, Raw Sienna, Ultra. Blue, and Lemon Yel. Mix Payne's Grey and Lemon Yellow for Bright Green leaves.

DRAMATIC ROSES. This is the same rose as on the preceding page but with the colors and values changed. This is something you can try for variety in color. Lay in the dark rose first; use very little White, only in the edges of petals and the highlight on cup of rose. Add a speck of Blue in the shadows. The background is Cobalt Blue, Raw Sienna, Cad. Red Medium, and White. Dark roses: Alizarin Crimson, Yellow, and Ultra. Blue. Pale pink roses: Rose Red, Yellow Ochre, and White. Leaves: Burnt Sienna, Lemon Yellow, Raw Sienna, and Ultra. Blue.

SUNBEAM ROSES. I put a sunbeam behind these, mixed mostly of Yel. Ochre and White. The roses are Rose Red, White, and a little Cad. Yellow Medium. Brown leaves: Burnt Sienna, Viridian, and Cad. Yel. Medium. Add this for reflection to the pitcher on the same side. Green leaves: Same color but more Green and White is added. Use some Burnt Sienna in the dark centers with a little Yellow. Palette: Viridian, Cad. Yel. Medium, Cad. Red Medium, Alizarin, Cob. Blue, Yel. Ochre, Rose Red, Cad. Lemon, Red, and Burnt Sienna.

These white roses have Rose Red centers with cool Gray shadows around the petals. I painted this to show water in the vase. Note how stems look larger in water than out of it. This took a lot of careful observation, also. Try this for practice, it is easier after a few tries at it. Set up your own vase of water and study it. The more you paint—the more you learn. I started painting when a child and just couldn't stop. If you want to be a good artist, be dedicated to your work. If you paint for pleasure just enjoy yourself, and you might even sell one.

COLOR SLIDES from the Walter Foster "HOW TO DRAW" BOOKS

NEW 35MM COLOR SLIDES NOW AVAILABLE

FIVE SLIDES PER SET $1.75

(Slides match page numbers in the books, as listed here.)

This is Slide Set #100-A

Book #4 — OIL PAINTING (CLOUDS)
Set A Set B Set C

Book #7 — FLOWERS
Set A
4/5 - Fuchsias
10/11 - Poppies
16/17 (cover) - Moss Roses
18/19 - Hibiscus
30 - Gladiolus

Book #8 — LANDSCAPES
Set A
8/9 - Robert Wood
10/11 - Leon Franks
14/15 - Hanson Puthuff
16/17 - Nell Walker Warner
20/21 - Robert Wood

Book #15 — PORTRAITS IN OIL
Set A
4/5 - Child
6/7 - Old Lady in Bonnet
16/17 - Young Woman
26/27 - Chinese Man
28/29 - Man

Book #52 — STILL LIFE
Set A
6/7 - Ranunculus
10/11 - Roses
20/21 - Coffee Pot
22/23 - Gourds
26/27 - Oriental Arrangement
Set B
9 - Copper Pot & Fruit
12/13 - Silver Pitcher
16/17 - Kettle & Wine Bottle
18/19 - Bottle & Fruit
24/25 - Onions
Set C
2/3 - Flowers
5 - Red Vase
9 - Copper Pot
15 - Vegetables
28/29 - Bowl of Fruit

Book #56 — MIXING COLORS
Set A
7 - Boat
12 - Flowers
15 - The Prayer
23 - Sea Cliffs
26 - New England Farm

Book #66 — ROBERT WOOD
Set A (SEASCAPES)
7 - Breakers
12 - Carmel by the Sea
13 - Laguna Rocks
17 - Surf
20 - Sunset

Set B (LANDSCAPES)
4 - Guadalupe River (Texas)
6 - Evening Desert
24 - Texas Spanish Oak
27 - Catskill Mountains
29 - Majectic Grand Tetons

Set C (LANDSCAPES)
5 - Lake Tahoe - Jeffrey Pines
25 - Carsons Peak (Sierras)
28 - Mountain Sunrise
30 - Natural Bridge (Ariz.)
Back cover - Winter Mt.

Book #72 — HEADS
4/5 - Tiare Tahiti
8/9 - Portrait of Lynn
12/13 - The Gypsy Baron
16/17 (cover) - Sugar & Spice
20/21 - Girl in the Red Pareau

Book #75 — CLAUDE PARSONS
Set A
16/17 (cover) - Matilija Poppies
21 - Yellow Cannas
25 - Cosmos
29 - Chrysanthemums
13 (back cover) - Roses

Book #79 — TECHNIQUES
Set A
4 - Pumpkins
8 - Onions
9 - Blue Bowl & Fruit
12 - Sandy's Portrait
20 - Yellow Bowl
Set B
3 - Pitcher
16/17 - Copper - Silver - Brass - Pewter
25 - Roses
28 - Fruit
29 - Watermelon

Book #80 — HORSES & RIDERS
Set A
12 - Covered Wagons
13 - Stagecoach
16/17 (cover) - The Bank Robbers
24/25 - Indian Raid
28/29 - The Stampede

Book #82 — NELL WALKER WARNER
Set A
4/5 - Fuchsia
9 - Fishing Boat
12/13 - Hawaiian Flowers
16/17 (cover) - Roses
24/25 - Shasta Daisies

Book #83 — SEA IN ACTION
8/9 - Cave
12/13 - White Foam
20/21 - Surf on Rocky Shores
24/25 - Sunset
28/29 - Surf by Moonlight

Book #91 — SKETCHES ABROAD
Set A
5 - Swiss Chalet
8 - Bridge Near Moulins
12 - Sacre-Coeur
13 - Street in Paris
28 - Cafe in Blois
Set B
16/17 - Amsterdam
20 - London - Variations on a Theme
21 - The Champs Elysees
24/25 (cover) - Innsbruck Golden Roof
29 - Berne Clock Tower

Book #92 — FRUIT & VEGETABLES
Set A
8/9 - Pineapple
12/13 - Four Studies
20/21 - Vegetables
24/25 - Copper Teapot
28/29 - Melon & Wine Bottle

Book #93 — MOODS IN OILS
Set A
5 - Canyon Walls
12 - High Fall
16/17 (cover) - Rock Towers
20 - Street in Patzcuaro
28/29 - The Grand Canyon

Book #96 — THE NUDE
Set A
13—16/17—21 (cover)
25—Back cover

Book #98 — BOATS
Set A
8 - Running Before the Wind
16/17 - Wind and Spray
28 - Sailing Trawlers
29 - A Hazy Day
Back cover - Full Sail

Book #100 — OIL PAINTING NO. 2
Set A
2/3 - Flowers
4 - Portugal Coast
10/11 (cover) - Doorway
16/17 - Sea in Action
22/23 - Full Sail
Set B
6/7 - Zinnias
18/19 - Fall Glory
20/21 - Fishing Boats
24/25 - California Hills
26/27 - French Villa
Set C
5 - Italian Castle
8 - Dutch Fishing Boat
9 - French Coast
13 - French Peasant Home
28/29 - Beached

Book #101 — SUNSETS
Set A
5 - Crimson Clouds
13 - Sunset and Surf
16/17 (cover) - Golden Reflections
21 - Indian Summer Sky
24/25 - Reflections on Wet Sand

BOOK #110 — SEA POWER
Set A
11 - Foggy Coast
12/13 - Calm Sea
14/15 - Open Sea
22/23 - Floating Foam
26/27 - Wave Movements

Book #111 — RED BARNS, ETC.
Set A
3 (cover) - Little Red Barn
5 - Rain - Washed
8 - Laguna Breakers
12 - After the Rain
16/17 - Radiant Afterglow
Set B
4 - Thunder Storm
9 - Carmel
13 - Golden Beauty
20 - Arizona Autumn
28 - Grandpa's White Barn
Set C
21 - Laguna Sunset
24 - Lone Cypress
25 - Big Sur
29 - Sea Lion Cave
7 (back cover) - Harbor Scene

Book #113 — 32 LESSONS IN OIL
Set A
7 - Smoke Trees
17 - Spring in Arizona
25 - Monument Valley
26 - Spring in the Desert
28 - Red Rock Panorama
Set B
21 - Deep Forest
23 - View of Cochise Head
30 - Laguna Breakers
31 - Oregon Coast
34 - Snow in White Mountains
Set C
5 - Autumn Valley
8 - New England Monarch
10 - The Matterhorn
12 - Yellow Thunder Country
14 - The Brenner Pass
Set D
9 - Old Cottonwood
11 - Oriental Spring
13 - June in the High Country
20 - Edge of Town
22 - Pastureland of the Navajos
Set E
16 - Oak Creek Canyon
18/19 - Trees
24 - The Grand Tetons
27 - California Meadow
29 - Muir Woods